M000107446

Slouchy Beanies
and Headwraps

2   4   6   9   12   14   16   19   22   24

LEISURE ARTS, INC. • Little Rock, Arkansas

SEED STITCH BEANIE

 **EASY**

SHOPPING LIST

Yarn (Medium Weight)

[3.5 ounces, 210 yards
(100 grams, 192 meters) per skein]:

☐ Grey - One skein

☐ Pink - One skein

Knitting Needles

16" (40.5 cm) Circular needles,

☐ Size 6 (4 mm) **and**

☐ Size 8 (5 mm)

or sizes needed for gauge

Double pointed needles,

☐ Size 8 (5 mm)

Additional Supplies

☐ Marker

☐ Yarn needle

☐ Tapestry needle

☐ ½" (12 mm) Buttons - 2

SIZE INFORMATION

Small/Medium {Large/X-Large}

Fits Head Circumference:

19{21}"/48.5{53.5} cm

Size Note: We have printed the
instructions for the sizes in different
colors to make it easier for you to find:

• Size Small/Medium in Blue

• Size Large/X-Large in Pink

Instructions in Black apply to both
sizes.

GAUGE INFORMATION

With larger size circular knitting
  needle, in Seed Stitch,
  16 sts and 28 rnds = 4" (10 cm)

TECHNIQUES USED

Knit increase *(Figs. 14a & b,
  page 29)*

Purl increase *(Fig. 15, page 29)*

K2 tog *(Fig. 16, page 30)*

K3 tog *(Fig. 18, page 30)*

INSTRUCTIONS
RIBBING

With smaller size circular knitting
needle and Pink, cast on 96{104} sts;
place a marker to mark the beginning
of the rnd *(see Using Circular
Knitting Needles and Markers,
page 27)*.

Rnd 1 (Right side): (K1, P1) around.

Repeat Rnd 1 until Ribbing measures
approximately 1½" (4 cm) from
cast on edge, increasing 25{17}
sts evenly spaced on last rnd *(see
Increasing Evenly, page 28)*: 121 sts.

BODY

Change to larger size circular knitting
needle.

Rnd 1: With Grey, knit around.

Rnd 2: P1, (K1, P1) around.

Rnd 3: K1, (P1, K1) around.

Repeat Rnds 2 and 3 for Seed Stitch
until piece measures approximately
6{7}"/15{18} cm from cast on edge,
ending by working Rnd 3.

SHAPING

Change to double pointed needles
when there are too few stitches to use
a circular needle *(see Using Double
Pointed Knitting Needles, page 28)*.

Rnd 1: P1, ★ (K1, P1) 3 times, K3 tog,
P1; repeat from ★ around: 97 sts.

Rnd 2: (K1, P1) 3 times, K3, ★ P1, (K1,
P1) twice, K3; repeat from ★ around.

Rnd 3: P1, (K1, P1) around.

Rnd 4: ★ (K1, P1) 3 times, K2 tog;
repeat from ★ around to last st, K1:
85 sts.

Rnd 5: P1, ★ (K1, P1) twice, K2, P1; repeat from ★ around.

Rnd 6: (K1, P1) 3 times, K2, ★ P1, (K1, P1) twice, K2; repeat from ★ around.

Rnd 7: P1, ★ (K1, P1) twice, K2 tog, P1; repeat from ★ around: 73 sts.

Rnd 8: (K1, P1) twice, K3, ★ P1, K1, P1, K3; repeat from ★ around.

Rnd 9: P1, (K1, P1) around.

Rnd 10: ★ (K1, P1) twice, K2 tog; repeat from ★ around to last st, K1: 61 sts.

Rnd 11: P1, ★ K1, P1, K2, P1; repeat from ★ around.

Rnd 12: (K1, P1) twice, K2, ★ P1, K1, P1, K2; repeat from ★ around.

Rnd 13: P1, ★ K1, P1, K2 tog, P1; repeat from ★ around: 49 sts.

Rnd 14: K1, (P1, K3) around.

Rnd 15: P1, (K1, K2 tog, P1) around: 37 sts.

Rnd 16: K1, (P1, K2) around.

Rnd 17: P1, (K2 tog, P1) around: 25 sts.

Rnd 18: Knit around.

Rnd 19: K1, K2 tog around: 13 sts.

Cut yarn leaving an 8" (20.5 cm) length for sewing. ◼️ Thread yarn needle with end and slip remaining sts onto yarn needle; pull **tightly** to close and secure end.

With Pink and using photo as a guide for placement, sew buttons to Ribbing.

RIBBED BEANIE

 **EASY**

SHOPPING LIST

Yarn (Medium Weight)
[3.5 ounces, 210 yards
(100 grams, 192 meters) per skein]:
☐ 1{2} skein(s)

Knitting Needles
16" (40.5 cm) Circular needles,
☐ Size 6 (4 mm) **and**
☐ Size 8 (5 mm)
or sizes needed for gauge
Double pointed needles,
☐ Size 8 (5 mm)

Additional Supplies
☐ Marker
☐ Yarn needle

SIZE INFORMATION

Small/Medium {Large/X-Large}
Fits Head Circumference:
19{21}"/48.5{53.5} cm

Size Note: We have printed the
instructions for the sizes in different
colors to make it easier for you to find:
• Size Small/Medium in Blue
• Size Large/X-Large in Pink
Instructions in Black apply to both
sizes.

GAUGE INFORMATION

With larger size circular knitting
needle, in Stockinette Stitch,
18 sts and 24 rnds = 4" (10 cm)

TECHNIQUES USED

- Knit increase (*Figs. 14a & b,*
  page 29)
- Purl increase (*Fig. 15, page 29*)
- K2 tog (*Fig. 16, page 30*)
- K3 tog (*Fig. 18, page 30*)

INSTRUCTIONS
RIBBING

With smaller size circular knitting
needle, cast on 94{104} sts; place a
marker to mark the beginning of the
rnd (*see Using Circular Knitting
Needles and Markers, page 27*).

Rnd 1 (Right side)**:** (K1, P1) around.

Repeat Rnd 1 until Ribbing measures
approximately 2" (5 cm) from cast on
edge, increasing 18{22} sts evenly
spaced on last rnd (***see Increasing
Evenly, page 28***): 112{126} sts.

BODY

Change to larger size circular knitting
needle.

Rnd 1: (K5, P2, K2, P1, K2, P2) around.

Rnd 2: Knit around.

Repeat Rnds 1 and 2 for pattern
until piece measures approximately
8{8½}"/20.5{21.5} cm from cast on
edge, ending by working Rnd 2.

SHAPING

Change to double pointed knitting
needles when there are too few
stitches to use a circular needle
(*see Using Double Pointed Knitting
Needles, page 28*).

Rnd 1: (K5, P2, K2, P1, K2, K2 tog)
around: 104{117} sts.

Rnd 2: Knit around.

Rnd 3: (K5, P2, K2, P1, K1, K2 tog)
around: 96{108} sts.

Rnd 4: Knit around.

Rnd 5: (K5, P2, K2, P1, K2 tog) around:
88{99} sts.

Rnd 6: Knit around.

Rnd 7: (K5, P2, K2, K2 tog) around: 80{90} sts.

Rnd 8: Knit around.

Rnd 9: (K5, P2, K1, K2 tog) around: 72{81} sts.

Rnd 10: Knit around.

Rnd 11: (K5, P2, K2 tog) around: 64{72} sts.

Rnd 12: Knit around.

Rnd 13: (K5, K3 tog) around: 48{54} sts.

Rnd 14: Knit around.

Rnd 15: (K3, K3 tog) around: 32{36} sts.

Rnd 16: Knit around.

Rnd 17: (K2, K2 tog) around: 24{27} sts.

Rnd 18: Knit around.

Rnd 19: K3 tog around: 8{9} sts.

Rnd 20: Knit around.

Cut yarn leaving an 8" (20.5 cm) length for sewing. 🎥 Thread yarn needle with end and slip remaining sts onto yarn needle; pull **tightly** to close and secure end.

TWISTY CABLES BEANIE

SHOPPING LIST

Yarn (Medium Weight)

[3 ounces, 185 yards
(85 grams, 170 meters) per skein]:

☐ One skein

Knitting Needles

16" (40.5 cm) Circular needles,

☐ Size 7 (4.5 mm) **and**

☐ Size 9 (5.5 mm)

or sizes needed for gauge

Double pointed needles,

☐ Size 9 (5.5 mm)

Additional Supplies

☐ Marker

☐ Cable needle

☐ Yarn needle

SIZE INFORMATION

Small/Medium {Large/X-Large}

Fits Head Circumference:

19{21}"/48.5{53.5} cm

Size Note: We have printed the
instructions for the sizes in different
colors to make it easier for you to find:

• Size Small/Medium in Blue

• Size Large/X-Large in Pink

Instructions in Black apply to both
sizes.

GAUGE INFORMATION

With larger size circular knitting
needle, in Stockinette Stitch,
16 sts and 22 rnds = 4" (10 cm)

TECHNIQUES USED

■ M1P (*Fig. 13, page 29*)

■ K2 tog (*Fig. 16, page 30*)

■ Slip 1 as if to **knit**, K1, PSSO
(*Figs. 19a & b, page 30*)

■ P2 tog (*Fig. 21, page 31*)

——— STITCH GUIDE ———

■ **LEFT TWIST** (*abbreviated LT*)
(uses 2 sts)

Working **behind** first stitch on left
needle, knit into the **back** of second
stitch (*Fig. 1a*) making sure **not** to
drop stitches off, then knit the first
stitch (*Fig. 1b*) letting both stitches
drop off the left needle.

Fig. 1a

Fig. 1b

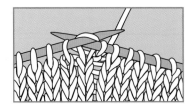

■ **RIGHT TWIST** (*abbreviated RT*)
(uses 2 sts)

Knit second stitch on left needle
(*Fig. 2a*) making sure **not** to drop
stitches off, then knit the first stitch
(*Fig. 2b*) letting both stitches drop off
the left needle.

Fig. 2a   **Fig. 2b**

■ **CABLE 6 BACK**
(*abbreviated C6B*)
(uses next 6 sts)

Slip next 3 sts onto cable needle
and hold in **back** of work, K3 from
left needle, K3 from cable needle.

INSTRUCTIONS
RIBBING

With smaller size circular knitting needle, cast on 96{108} sts; place a marker to mark the beginning of the rnd 📹 *(see Using Circular Knitting Needles and Markers, page 27)*.

Rnd 1 (Right side)**:** (K2, P2) around.

Rnd 2: (LT, P2) around.

Rnds 3 and 4: (K2, P2) around.

Rnds 5-8: Repeat Rnds 2-4 once, then repeat Rnd 2 once **more**.

Rnd 9: ★ K2, P2, (K2, P1, M1P, P1) twice; repeat from ★ around: 112{126} sts.

BODY

Change to larger size circular knitting needle.

Rnds 1 and 2: (K6, P8) around.

Rnd 3: (C6B, P8) around.

Rnd 4: (K6, P8) around.

Rnd 5: (K4, RT, P8) around.

Rnd 6: (K6, P8) around.

Rnd 7: (K3, RT, K1, P8) around.

Rnd 8: (K6, P8) around.

Rnd 9: (K2, RT twice, P8) around.

Rnd 10: (K6, P8) around.

Rnd 11: (K1, RT twice, K1, P8) around.

Rnd 12: (K6, P8) around.

Rnd 13: (RT twice, K2, P8) around.

Rnd 14: (K6, P8) around.

Rnd 15: (K1, RT, K3, P8) around.

Rnd 16: (K6, P8) around.

Rnd 17: (RT, K4, P8) around.

Rnds 18-20: (K6, P8) around.

Rnd 21: (C6B, P8) around.

Rnds 22-26: (K6, P8) around.

Rnds 27 thru 32{38}: Repeat Rnds 21-26, 1{2} time(s).

SHAPING

Change to double pointed needles when there are too few stitches to use a circular needle 📹 *(see Using Double Pointed Knitting Needles, page 28)*.

Rnd 1: (C6B, P2 tog, P4, P2 tog) around: 96{108} sts.

Rnds 2-4: (K6, P6) around.

Rnd 5: (K6, P2 tog, P2, P2 tog) around: 80{90} sts.

Rnd 6: (K6, P4) around.

Rnd 7: (C6B, P4) around.

Rnd 8: (K6, P4) around.

Rnd 9: (K6, P2 tog twice) around: 64{72} sts.

Rnds 10 and 11: (K6, P2) around.

Rnd 12: ★ K1, slip 1 as if to **knit**, K1, PSSO, K2 tog, K1, P2; repeat from ★ around: 48{54} sts.

Rnds 13 and 14: (K4, P2) around.

Rnd 15: (K2 tog twice, P2) around: 32{36} sts.

Rnd 16: (RT, P2) around.

Rnd 17: (K2, P2 tog) around: 24{27} sts.

Cut yarn leaving an 8" (20.5 cm) length for sewing. 📹 Thread yarn needle with end and slip remaining sts onto yarn needle; pull **tightly** to close and secure end.

LACY BEANIE

Shown on page 11.

 **EASY**

SHOPPING LIST

Yarn (Medium Weight)
[3 ounces, 185 yards
(85 grams, 170 meters) per skein]:
☐ 1{2} skein(s)

Knitting Needles
16" (40.5 cm) Circular needles as
indicated below **or** sizes needed
for gauge:
Size Small/Medium:
☐ Size 7 (4.5 mm) **and**
☐ Size 8 (5 mm)
Size Large/X-Large:
☐ Size 7 (4.5 mm) **and**
Size 9 (5.5 mm)
Double pointed needles as
indicated below:
Size Small/Medium:
☐ Size 8 (5 mm)
Size Large/X-Large:
☐ Size 9 (5.5 mm)

Additional Supplies
☐ Marker
☐ Yarn needle

SIZE INFORMATION
Small/Medium {Large/X-Large}
Fits Head Circumference:
19{21}"/48.5{53.5} cm

Size Note: We have printed the
instructions for the sizes in different
colors to make it easier for you to find:
• Size Small/Medium in Blue
• Size Large/X-Large in Pink
Instructions in Black apply to both
sizes.

GAUGE INFORMATION
With larger size circular knitting
needle, in Stockinette Stitch,
18{16} sts and 24{22} rnds =
4" (10 cm)

TECHNIQUES USED
 YO (*Fig. 9, page 28*)
 Knit increase (*Figs. 14a & b,
page 29*)
 Purl increase (*Fig. 15, page 29*)
 K2 tog (*Fig. 16, page 30*)
 K3 tog (*Fig. 18, page 30*)
 Slip 1 as if to knit, K1, PSSO
(*Figs. 19a & b, page 30*)
 Slip 1 as if to knit, K2 tog, PSSO
(*Fig. 20, page 31*)

INSTRUCTIONS
RIBBING
With smaller size circular knitting
needle, cast on 94{102} sts; place a
marker to mark the beginning of the
rnd (*see Using Circular Knitting
Needles and Markers, page 27*).

Rnd 1 (Right side)**:** (K1, P1) around.

Repeat Rnd 1 until Ribbing measures
approximately 1¾" (4.5 cm) from
cast on edge, increasing 16{8} sts
evenly spaced on last rnd (*see
Increasing Evenly, page 28*): 110 sts.

BODY
Change to larger size circular knitting
needle.

Rnd 1: K4, K2 tog, YO, K1, YO, slip 1 as
if to **knit**, K1, PSSO, ★ K6, K2 tog, YO,
K1, YO, slip 1 as if to **knit**, K1, PSSO;
repeat from ★ around to last 2 sts, K2.

Rnd 2: Knit around.

Rnd 3: K3, K2 tog, YO, K3, YO, slip 1 as
if to **knit**, K1, PSSO, ★ K4, K2 tog, YO,
K3, YO, slip 1 as if to **knit**, K1, PSSO;
repeat from ★ around to last st, K1.

Rnd 4: Knit around.

Rnd 5: ★ K2, K2 tog, YO, K5, YO, slip 1 as if to **knit**, K1, PSSO; repeat from ★ around.

Rnd 6: Knit around.

Rnd 7: K3, YO, slip 1 as if to **knit**, K1, PSSO, K3, K2 tog, YO, ★ K4, YO, slip 1 as if to **knit**, K1, PSSO, K3, K2 tog, YO; repeat from ★ around to last st, K1.

Rnd 8: Knit around.

Rnd 9: K4, YO, slip 1 as if to **knit**, K1, PSSO, K1, K2 tog, YO, ★ K6, YO, slip 1 as if to **knit**, K1, PSSO, K1, K2 tog, YO; repeat from ★ around to last 2 sts, K2.

Rnd 10: Knit around.

Rnd 11: K5, YO, K3 tog, YO, ★ K8, YO, K3 tog, YO; repeat from ★ around to last 3 sts, K3.

Rnd 12: Knit around.

Rnds 13-36: Repeat Rnds 1-12 twice.

SHAPING

Change to double pointed needles when there are too few stitches to use a circular needle 🎥 *(see Using Double Pointed Knitting Needles, page 28).*

Rnd 1: K3, K3 tog, YO, K1, YO, slip 1 as if to **knit**, K2 tog, PSSO, ★ K4, K3 tog, YO, K1, YO, slip 1 as if to **knit**, K2 tog, PSSO; repeat from ★ around to last st, K1: 90 sts.

Rnd 2: Knit around.

Rnd 3: Remove marker, with yarn in back, slip 1 as if to **purl**, replace marker on right needle, K1, K2 tog, YO, K3, YO, slip 1 as if to **knit**, K1, PSSO, ★ K2, K2 tog, YO, K3, YO, slip 1 as if to **knit**, K1, PSSO; repeat from ★ around to last st, K1.

Rnd 4: Knit around.

Rnd 5: ★ K2 tog, YO, K1, slip 1 as if to **knit**, K2 tog, PSSO, K1, YO, slip 1 as if to **knit**, K1, PSSO; repeat from ★ around: 70 sts.

Rnd 6: Knit around.

Rnd 7: K2, YO, slip 1 as if to **knit**, K2 tog, PSSO, ★ YO, K4, YO, slip 1 as if to **knit**, K2 tog, PSSO; repeat from ★ around to last 2 sts, YO, K2.

Rnd 8: Knit around.

Rnd 9: K2, slip 1 as if to **knit**, K2 tog, PSSO, ★ K4, slip 1 as if to **knit**, K2 tog, PSSO; repeat from ★ around to last 2 sts, K2: 50 sts.

Rnd 10: Knit around.

Rnd 11: K1, slip 1 as if to **knit**, K2 tog, PSSO, ★ K2, slip 1 as if to **knit**, K2 tog, PSSO; repeat from ★ around to last st, K1: 30 sts.

Rnd 12: Knit around.

Rnd 13: ★ Slip 1 as if to **knit**, K2 tog, PSSO; repeat from ★ around: 10 sts.

Rnd 14: Knit around.

Cut yarn leaving an 8" (20.5 cm) length for sewing. 🎥 Thread yarn needle with end and slip remaining sts onto yarn needle; pull **tightly** to close and secure end.

BASIC BEANIE

 **EASY**

SHOPPING LIST

Yarn (Medium Weight) 🔢 **4** MEDIUM
[2.5 ounces, 153 yards
(70 grams, 140 meters) per skein]:
☐ 1{2} skein(s)

Knitting Needles
16" (40.5 cm) Circular needles,
☐ Size 7 (4.5 mm) **and**
☐ Size 8 (5 mm)
   or sizes needed for gauge
Double pointed needles,
☐ Size 8 (5 mm)

Additional Supplies
☐ Marker
☐ Yarn needle
☐ Sewing needle
☐ Matching thread
☐ 1¼" (32 mm) Button

SIZE INFORMATION

Small/Medium {Large/X-Large}

Fits Head Circumference:
19{21}"/48.5{53.5} cm

Size Note: We have printed the
instructions for the sizes in different
colors to make it easier for you to find:
• Size Small/Medium in Blue
• Size Large/X-Large in Pink
Instructions in Black apply to both
sizes.

GAUGE INFORMATION

With larger size circular knitting
needle, in Stockinette Stitch,
18 sts and 24 rows = 4" (10 cm)

TECHNIQUES USED

🎥 Knit increase *(Figs. 14a & b,*
page 29)
🎥 Purl increase *(Fig. 15, page 29)*
🎥 Slip 1 as if to **knit**, K1, PSSO
(Figs. 19a & b, page 30)

INSTRUCTIONS
BAND

With smaller size circular knitting
needle, cast on 90{98} sts.

Row 1 (Right side)**:** Working in rows,
bind off 8 sts in knit for button loop,
knit across: 82{90} sts.

Rows 2-11: Knit across.

Row 12: Bind off 6 sts in knit for flap,
knit across increasing 6 sts evenly
spaced across *(see Increasing Evenly,*
page 28); place a marker to mark
the beginning of the rnd 🎥 *(see*
Using Circular Knitting Needles and
Markers, page 27): 82{90} sts.

BODY

Change to larger size circular knitting
needle.

Rnd 1 (Right side)**:** Knit around
increasing 18{10} sts evenly spaced:
100 sts.

Work in Stockinette Stitch (knit
every rnd) until piece measures
approximately 7{8}"/18{20.5} cm from
cast on edge.

SHAPING

Change to double pointed needles
when there are too few stitches to use
a circular needle 🎥 *(see Using Double*
Pointed Knitting Needles, page 28).

Rnd 1: (Slip 1 as if to **knit**, K1, PSSO,
K8) around: 90 sts.

Rnd 2 AND ALL EVEN-NUMBERED
RNDS: Knit around.

Rnd 3: (Slip 1 as if to **knit**, K1, PSSO,
K7) around: 80 sts.

Rnd 5: (Slip 1 as if to **knit**, K1, PSSO,
K6) around: 70 sts.

Rnd 7: (Slip 1 as if to **knit**, K1, PSSO, K5) around: 60 sts.

Rnd 9: (Slip 1 as if to **knit**, K1, PSSO, K4) around: 50 sts.

Rnd 11: (Slip 1 as if to **knit**, K1, PSSO, K3) around: 40 sts.

Rnd 13: (Slip 1 as if to **knit**, K1, PSSO, K2) around: 30 sts.

Rnd 15: (Slip 1 as if to **knit**, K1, PSSO, K1) around: 20 sts.

Rnd 17: (Slip st as if to **knit**, K1, PSSO) around: 10 sts.

Rnd 18: Knit around.

Cut yarn leaving an 8" (20.5 cm) length for sewing.  Thread yarn needle with end and slip remaining sts onto yarn needle; pull **tightly** to close and secure end.

Thread yarn needle with beginning end and secure at top corner of Band to form button loop.

Sew button to Band opposite button loop.

CABLES BEANIE

SHOPPING LIST

Yarn (Medium Weight) 🪢 **4**

[3.5 ounces, 209 yards
(100 grams, 191 meters) per skein]:

☐ One skein

Knitting Needles

16" (40.5 cm) Circular needles,

☐ Size 7 (4.5 mm) **and**

☐ Size 8 (5 mm)

or sizes needed for gauge

Double pointed needles,

☐ Size 8 (5 mm)

Additional Supplies

☐ Marker

☐ Cable needle

☐ Yarn needle

SIZE INFORMATION

Small/Medium {Large/X-Large}

Fits Head Circumference:

19{21}"/48.5{53.5} cm

Size Note: We have printed the
instructions for the sizes in different
colors to make it easier for you to find:

• Size Small/Medium in Blue
• Size Large/X-Large in Pink

Instructions in Black apply to both
sizes.

GAUGE INFORMATION

With larger size circular knitting
needle, in Stockinette Stitch,
18 sts and 24 rows = 4" (10 cm)

TECHNIQUES USED

📹 Knit increase *(Figs. 14a & b,
page 29)*

📹 Purl increase *(Fig. 15, page 29)*

📹 K2 tog tbl *(Fig. 17, page 30)*

📹 P2 tog *(Fig. 21, page 31)*

📹 P3 tog *(Fig. 22, page 31)*

——— STITCH GUIDE ———

📹 **CABLE 4 FRONT**

(abbreviated C4F)

(uses next 4 sts)

Slip next 2 sts onto cable needle
and hold in **front** of work, K2 from
left needle, K2 from cable needle.

INSTRUCTIONS
RIBBING

With smaller size circular knitting
needle, cast on 96{104} sts; place a
marker to mark the beginning of the
rnd 📹 *(see Using Circular Knitting
Needles and Markers, page 27)*.

Rnd 1 (Right side)**:** (K2, P2) around.

Repeat Rnd 1 until Ribbing
measures approximately 1½" (4 cm)
from cast on edge, increasing
14{16} sts evenly spaced on last rnd
(see Increasing Evenly, page 28):
110{120} sts.

BODY

Change to larger size circular knitting
needle.

Rnds 1-4: ★ P7{8}, K4; repeat from ★
around.

Rnd 5: ★ P7{8}, C4F; repeat from ★
around.

Repeat Rnds 1-5 for pattern until
piece measures approximately
7{8}"/18{20.5} cm from cast on edge,
ending by working Rnd 4.

SHAPING

Change to double pointed needles
when there are too few stitches to
use a circular needle 📹 *(see Using
Double Pointed Knitting Needles,
page 28)*.

Rnd 1: ★ P2 tog, P3{4}, P2 tog, C4F;
repeat from ★ around: 90{100} sts.

Rnds 2-4: ★ P5{6}, K4; repeat from ★ around.

Rnd 5: ★ P2 tog, P1{2}, P2 tog, K4; repeat from ★ around: 70{80} sts.

Rnd 6: ★ P3{4} C4F; repeat from ★ around.

Rnds 7 and 8: ★ P3{4}, K4; repeat from ★ around.

Size Small/Medium ONLY
Rnd 9: (P3 tog, K4) around: 50 sts.

Size Large/X-Large ONLY
Rnd 9: (P2 tog twice, K4) around: 60 sts.

Both Sizes
Rnd 10: ★ P1{2}, K4; repeat from ★ around.

Rnd 11: ★ P1{2}, C4F; repeat from ★ around.

Rnd 12: ★ P1{2}, K2 tog tbl twice; repeat from ★ around: 30{40} sts.

Cut yarn leaving an 8" (20.5 cm) length for sewing. 🎥 Thread yarn needle with end and slip remaining sts onto yarn needle; pull **tightly** to close and secure end.

 **EASY**

SHOPPING LIST

Yarn (Medium Weight)

[5 ounces, 256 yards
(140 grams, 234 meters) per skein]:
☐ One skein

Knitting Needles

16" (40.5 cm) Circular needles,
☐ Size 7 (4.5 mm) **and**
☐ Size 8 (5 mm)
or sizes needed for gauge
Double pointed needles,
☐ Size 8 (5 mm)

Additional Supplies

☐ Marker
☐ Yarn needle

SIZE INFORMATION

Small/Medium {Large/X-Large}
Fits Head Circumference:
19{21}"/48.5{53.5} cm

Size Note: We have printed the
instructions for the sizes in different
colors to make it easier for you to find:
• Size Small/Medium in Blue
• Size Large/X-Large in Pink
Instructions in Black apply to both
sizes.

GAUGE INFORMATION

With larger size circular knitting
needle, in Stockinette Stitch,
17 sts and 23 rows = 4" (10 cm)

TECHNIQUES USED

■ Adding New Stitches
(*Figs. 11a & b, page 29*)
■ M1 (*Figs. 12a & b, page 29*)
■ Knit increase (*Figs. 14a & b,
page 29*)
■ Purl increase (*Fig. 15, page 29*)
■ K2 tog (*Fig. 16, page 30*)
■ K2 tog tbl (*Fig. 17, page 30*)
■ P2 tog (*Fig. 21, page 31*)

INSTRUCTIONS
VISOR

With smaller size circular knitting
needle and holding 2 strands of yarn
together, cast on 17 sts.

**Row 1 AND ALL ODD-NUMBERED
ROWS:** Purl across.

Row 2 (Right side - Increase row)**:**
(K1, M1) twice, knit across to last 2 sts,
(M1, K1) twice: 21 sts.

Row 3: Purl across.

Row 4: Knit across.

Row 5: Purl across.

Rows 6-11: Repeat Rows 2-5 once,
then repeat Rows 2 and 3 once **more**:
29 sts.

Rows 12-14: Repeat Rows 2-4: 33 sts.

Cut one strand, leaving a long end.

RIBBING

Rnd 1: With remaining strand,
add on 44{48} sts; place a marker to
mark the beginning of the rnd ■ (*see
Using Circular Knitting Needles and
Markers, page 27*): 77{81} sts.

Rnd 2: (K1, P1, knit increase) 11 times,
(K1, P1) around: 88{92} sts.

Rnd 3: (K1, P1) around.

Repeat Rnd 3 until Ribbing measures
approximately 1¾" (4.5 cm),
increasing 10{13} sts evenly spaced
on last rnd (*see Increasing Evenly,
page 28*): 98{105} sts.

BODY

Change to larger size circular knitting needle.

Rnds 1 and 2: (K2, P5) around.

Rnds 3-5: Knit around.

Rnds 6-35: Repeat Rnds 1-5, 6 times.

SHAPING

Change to double pointed needles when there are too few stitches to use a circular needle ▄◄ *(see Using Double Pointed Knitting Needles, page 28).*

Rnd 1: (K2, P3, P2 tog) around: 84{90} sts.

Rnd 2: (K2, P4) around.

Rnds 3 and 4: Knit around.

Rnd 5: (K4, K2 tog) around: 70{75} sts.

Rnds 6 and 7: (K2, P3) around.

Rnd 8: Knit around.

Rnd 9: (K3, K2 tog) around: 56{60} sts.

Rnd 10: Knit around.

Rnds 11 and 12: (K2, P2) around.

Rnd 13: (K2, K2 tog) around: 42{45} sts.

Rnds 14 and 15: Knit around.

Rnd 16: (K2, P1) around.

Rnd 17: (K2 tog, P1) around: 28{30} sts.

Rnd 18: Knit around.

Rnd 19: K2 tog tbl around: 14{15} sts.

Cut yarn leaving an 8" (20.5 cm) length for sewing. ▄◄ Thread yarn needle with end and slip remaining sts onto yarn needle; pull **tightly** to close and secure end.

LACY HEADWRAP

Shown on page 21.

Shown on page 21.

 **EASY**

SHOPPING LIST

Yarn (Medium Weight)

[3 ounces, 197 yards

(85 grams, 180 meters) per skein]:

☐ One skein

Knitting Needles

Straight needles,

☐ Size 8 (5 mm)

or size needed for gauge

Additional Supplies

☐ Marker

☐ Sewing needle

☐ Matching thread

☐ 1¼" (32 mm) Button

SIZE INFORMATION

Small/Medium {Large/X-Large}

Fits Head Circumference:

19{21}"/48.5{53.5} cm

Size Note: We have printed the instructions for the sizes in different colors to make it easier for you to find:

• Size Small/Medium in Blue

• Size Large/X-Large in Pink

Instructions in Black apply to both sizes.

GAUGE INFORMATION

In Stockinette Stitch,

18 sts and 24 rows = 4" (10 cm)

TECHNIQUES USED

- YO *(Fig. 9, page 28)*
- YO twice *(Fig. 10, page 28)*
- K2 tog *(Fig. 16, page 30)*
- K3 tog *(Fig. 18, page 30)*
- Slip 1 as if to knit, K1, PSSO *(Figs. 19a & b, page 30)*
- Slip 1 as if to knit, K2 tog, PSSO *(Fig. 20, page 31)*

STITCH GUIDE

LEFT TWIST *(abbreviated LT)* (uses 2 sts)

Working **behind** first stitch on left needle, knit into the **back** of second stitch *(Fig. 3a)* making sure **not** to drop stitches off, then knit the first stitch *(Fig. 3b)* letting both stitches drop off the left needle.

Fig. 3a

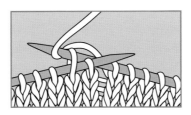

Fig. 3b

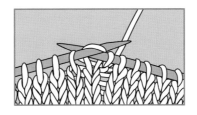

RIGHT TWIST *(abbreviated RT)* (uses 2 sts)

Knit second stitch on left needle *(Fig. 4a)* making sure **not** to drop stitches off, then knit the first stitch *(Fig. 4b)* letting both stitches drop off the left needle.

Fig. 4a

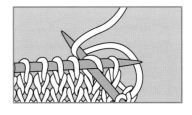

Fig. 4b

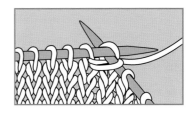

INSTRUCTIONS

FIRST END

Cast on 6 sts.

Row 1 (Right side)**:** Knit across.

Row 2: K1, P4, K1.

Row 3: K1, YO, LT, RT, YO, K1: 8 sts.

Row 4: K2, P4, K2.

Row 5: Knit across.

Row 6: K2, P4, K2.

Row 7: K2, YO, 📹 place a marker *(see Markers, page 27)*, LT, RT, YO, knit across: 10 sts.

Row 8: K2, purl across to last 2 sts, K2.

Row 9: Knit across.

Row 10: K2, purl across to last 2 sts, K2.

Row 11 (Increase row)**:** Knit across to marker, YO, slip marker, LT, RT, YO, knit across: 12 sts.

Row 12: K2, purl across to last 2 sts, K2.

Row 13: Knit across.

Row 14: K2, purl across to last 2 sts, K2.

Row 15-50: Repeat Rows 11-14, 9 times: 30 sts.

BODY

Row 1: Knit across to within 2 sts of marker, K2 tog, YO, slip marker, LT, RT, YO, slip 1 as if to **knit**, K1, PSSO, knit across.

Row 2: K2, purl across to last 2 sts, K2.

Row 3: Knit across.

Row 4: K2, purl across to last 2 sts, K2.

Repeat Rows 1-4 until piece measures approximately 13½{15½}"/ 34.5{39.5} cm from cast on edge, ending by working Row 4.

SECOND END

Row 1 (Decrease row)**:** Knit across to within 3 sts of marker, K3 tog, YO, slip marker, LT, RT, YO, slip 1 as if to **knit**, K2 tog, PSSO, knit across: 28 sts.

Row 2: K2, purl across to last 2 sts, K2.

Row 3: Knit across.

Row 4: K2, purl across to last 2 sts, K2.

Rows 5-36: Repeat Rows 1-4, 8 times: 12 sts.

Row 37: K1, K3 tog, remove marker, YO, LT, RT, YO, slip 1 as if to **knit**, K2 tog, PSSO, K1: 10 sts.

Row 38: K2, purl across to last 2 sts, K2.

Row 39: Knit across.

Row 40: K2, purl across to last 2 sts, K2.

Row 41: K3 tog, YO, LT, RT, YO, slip 1 as if to **knit**, K2 tog, PSSO: 8 sts.

Row 42: K2, P4, K2.

Row 43: Knit across.

Row 44: K2, P4, K2.

Row 45 (Buttonhole row)**:** K2 tog, K1, YO twice (**buttonhole made**), bind off next 2 sts, K2 tog: 6 sts.

Row 46: K1, P1, K1, P2, K1.

Bind off all sts in pattern.

Sew button to center of Row 15 of First End.

CABLE HEADWRAP

 **EASY**

SHOPPING LIST

Yarn (Medium Weight)

[1.75 ounces, 147 yards
(50 grams, 135 meters) per skein]:

☐ One skein

Knitting Needles

Straight needles,

☐ Size 8 (5 mm)

or size needed for gauge

Additional Supplies

☐ Sewing needle

☐ Matching thread

☐ 1½" (38 mm) Button

SIZE INFORMATION

Small/Medium {Large/X-Large}
Fits Head Circumference:
19{21}"/48.5{53.5} cm

Size Note: We have printed the
instructions for the sizes in different
colors to make it easier for you to
find:

• Size Small/Medium in Blue
• Size Large/X-Large in Pink
Instructions in Black apply to both
sizes.

GAUGE INFORMATION

In Stockinette Stitch,
18 sts and 24 rows = 4" (10 cm)

TECHNIQUES USED

📹 YO *(Fig. 9, page 28)*
📹 Double Increase *(page 29)*
📹 K2 tog *(Fig. 16, page 30)*
📹 K3 tog *(Fig.18, page 30)*
📹 P2 tog *(Fig. 21, page 31)*

INSTRUCTIONS
BODY

Cast on 25 sts.

Rows 1 and 2: K1, (P1, K1) across.

Row 3 (Right side): (K1, P1) twice,
double increase, (P3, double increase)
4 times, (P1, K1) twice: 35 sts.

Row 4: K1, P1, K2, P3, (K3, P3) 4 times,
K2, P1, K1.

Row 5: (K1, P1) twice, K3 tog, (P3,
K3 tog) 4 times, (P1, K1) twice: 25 sts.

Row 6: K1, P1, knit across to last 2 sts,
P1, K1.

Repeat Rows 3-6 for pattern until
piece measures approximately
19½{21½}"/49.5{54.5} cm from cast on
edge, ending by working Row 4.

FLAP

Row 1 (Buttonhole row): (K1, P1)
twice, (K3 tog, P3) twice, [K2, pass
second st on right needle over first
st, K1, pass second st on right needle
over first st, P1, pass second st on
right needle over first st (**buttonhole
made**)], P2, K3 tog, P3, K3 tog, (P1, K1)
twice: 24 sts.

Row 2: K1, P1, K 10, YO, K 10, P1, K1:
25 sts.

Row 3: (K1, P1) twice, P2 tog twice,
double increase, (P3, double increase)
twice, P2 tog twice, (P1, K1) twice:
27 sts.

Row 4: K1, P1, K2 tog twice, P3, (K3,
P3) twice, K2 tog twice, P1, K1: 23 sts.

Row 5: (K1, P1) twice, K3 tog, (P3,
K3 tog) twice, (P1, K1) twice: 17 sts.

Row 6: K1, P1, knit across to last 2 sts,
P1, K1.

Row 7: (K1, P1) twice, P2 tog twice, double increase, P2 tog twice, (P1, K1) twice: 15 sts.

Row 8: K1, P1, K2 tog twice, P3, K2 tog twice, P1, K1: 11 sts.

Row 9: (K1, P1) twice, K3 tog, (P1, K1) twice: 9 sts.

Row 10: K1, P1, knit across to last 2 sts, P1, K1.

Rows 11 and 12: K1, (P1, K1) across.

Bind Off Row: K1, ★ K2 tog, pass second st on right needle over first st; repeat from ★ across; cut yarn, pull end through last st.

Sew button to center of Row 12 of Body.

SPLIT HEADWRAP

 INTERMEDIATE

SHOPPING LIST

Yarn (Medium Weight) **MEDIUM 4**

**[1.75 ounces, 80 yards
(50 grams, 73 meters) per skein]:**

☐ 2 skeins

Knitting Needles

Straight needles,

☐ Size 7 (4.5 mm)

or size needed for gauge

Additional Supplies

☐ Stitch holder

☐ Yarn needle

SIZE INFORMATION

Small/Medium {Large/X-Large}

Fits Head Circumference:

19{21}"/48.5{53.5} cm

Size Note: We have printed the instructions for the sizes in different colors to make it easier for you to find:

• Size Small/Medium in Blue
• Size Large/X-Large in Pink

Instructions in Black apply to both sizes.

GAUGE INFORMATION

In pattern,

17 sts and 15 rows = 4" (10 cm)

TECHNIQUES USED

🎥 M1 (*Figs. 12a & b, page 29*)

🎥 P2 tog (*Fig. 21, page 31*)

INSTRUCTIONS
FIRST SECTION

Cast on 33 sts.

Row 1: Slip 1 as if to **knit**, (K1, P1) across.

Row 2 (Right side)**:** Slip 1 as if to **knit**, ★ P1, 🎥 knit st one row **below** next st (*Fig. 5*); repeat from ★ across to last 2 sts, P2.

Fig. 5

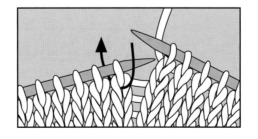

Repeat Rows 1 and 2 for pattern until piece measures approximately 5{6}"/12.5{15} cm from cast on edge, ending by working Row 2.

SPLIT

Both sides of Split are worked at the same time, using separate yarn for **each** side.

Row 1: Slip 1 as if to **knit**, K1, (P1, K1) 7 times, M1, slip 1 as if to **knit**; with second yarn, (K1, P1) across: 17 sts on **each** side.

Row 2: Slip 1 as if to **knit**, (P1, knit st one row **below** next st) across to last 2 sts, P2; with second yarn, slip 1 as if to **knit**, (P1, knit st one row **below** next st) across to last 2 sts, P2.

Row 3: Slip 1 as if to **knit**, (K1, P1) across; with second yarn, slip 1 as if to **knit**, (K1, P1) across.

Repeat Rows 2 and 3 for pattern, until piece measures approximately 13{14}"/33{35.5} cm from cast on edge, ending by working Row 2.

SECOND SECTION

Row 1: Slip 17 sts onto st holder, cut yarn from this half; with second yarn,  slip 1 as if to **knit**, K1, (P1, K1) 7 times, slip last st from left needle onto right needle as if to **purl**; slip sts from st holder onto empty needle (second half) and cross it **behind** first half being careful **not** to twist piece, move slipped st on right needle back onto left needle, P2 tog (last st from first half and first st from second half), (K1, P1) across: 33 sts.

Row 2: Slip 1 as if to **knit**, (P1, knit st one row **below** next st) across to last 2 sts, P2.

Row 3: Slip 1 as if to **knit**, (K1, P1) across.

Repeat Rows 2 and 3 for pattern until piece measures approximately 18{20}"/45.5{51} cm from cast on edge, ending by working Row 2.

Bind off all sts in pattern.

With **wrong** side together and being careful **not** to twist piece, sew cast on edge to bound off edge.

GENERAL INSTRUCTIONS

ABBREVIATIONS

C6B	Cable 6 Back	P	purl
C4F	Cable 4 Front	PSSO	pass slipped st over
cm	centimeters	Rnd(s)	Round(s)
LT	Left Twist	RT	Right Twist
K	knit	st(s)	stitch(es)
M1	Make one	tbl	through back loop
M1P	Make one purl	tog	together
mm	millimeters	YO	yarn over

SYMBOLS & TERMS

★ — work instructions following ★ as many **more** times as indicated in addition to the first time.

( ) or [ ] — work enclosed instructions **as many** times as specified by the number immediately following **or** contains explanatory remarks.

colon (:) — the number(s) given after a colon at the end of a row or round denote(s) the number of stitches you should have on that row or round.

Yarn Weight Symbol & Names	LACE ⓿ 0	SUPER FINE 1	FINE 2	LIGHT 3	MEDIUM 4	BULKY 5	SUPER BULKY 6
Type of Yarns in Category	Fingering, size 10 crochet thread	Sock, Fingering, Baby	Sport, Baby	DK, Light Worsted	Worsted, Afghan, Aran	Chunky, Craft, Rug	Bulky, Roving
Knit Gauge Range* in Stockinette St to 4" (10 cm)	33-40** sts	27-32 sts	23-26 sts	21-24 sts	16-20 sts	12-15 sts	6-11 sts
Advised Needle Size Range	000-1	1 to 3	3 to 5	5 to 7	7 to 9	9 to 11	11 and larger

*GUIDELINES ONLY: The chart above reflects the most commonly used gauges and needle sizes for specific yarn categories.

** Lace weight yarns are usually knitted on larger needles to create lacy openwork patterns. Accordingly, a gauge range is difficult to determine. Always follow the gauge stated in your pattern.

KNIT TERMINOLOGY	
UNITED STATES	INTERNATIONAL
gauge =	tension
bind off =	cast off
yarn over (YO) =	yarn forward (yfwd) **or** yarn around needle (yrn)

◼◻◻◻ BEGINNER		Projects for first-time knitters using basic knit and purl stitches. Minimal shaping.
◼◼◻◻ EASY		Projects using basic stitches, repetitive stitch patterns, simple color changes, and simple shaping and finishing.
◼◼◼◻ INTERMEDIATE		Projects with a variety of stitches, such as basic cables and lace, simple intarsia, double-pointed needles and knitting in the round needle techniques, mid-level shaping and finishing.
◼◼◼◼ EXPERIENCED		Projects using advanced techniques and stitches, such as short rows, fair isle, more intricate intarsia, cables, lace patterns, and numerous color changes.

KNITTING NEEDLES																		
U.S.	0	1	2	3	4	5	6	7	8	9	10	10½	11	13	15	17	19	35	50
U.K.	13	12	11	10	9	8	7	6	5	4	3	2	1	00	000	---	---	---	---
Metric - mm	2	2.25	2.75	3.25	3.5	3.75	4	4.5	5	5.5	6	6.5	8	9	10	12.75	15	19	25

GAUGE

Exact gauge is **essential** for proper size. Before beginning your project, make a sample swatch in the yarn and needles specified in the individual instructions. After completing the swatch, measure it, counting your stitches and rows/rounds carefully. If your swatch is larger or smaller than specified, **make another, changing needle size to get the correct gauge.** Keep trying until you find the size needles that will give you the specified gauge.

SIZING

To determine what size to make, measure around the crown of your head with a tape measure *(Fig. 6)*. As long as the Beanie is made from a yarn with elasticity, the fabric will have some give. You want the band to fit snugly, so choose the size closest to your measurement or slightly smaller. You can also adjust the band size by changing the needle size used for it, and therefore adjusting the gauge and the finished measurement.

Fig. 6

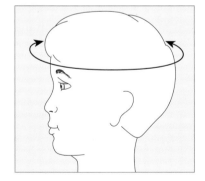

MARKERS

As a convenience to you, we have used markers to help distinguish the beginning of a round or a pattern. Place a marker as instructed. You may use a purchased marker or tie a length of contrasting color yarn around the needle. When you reach a marker on each round or row, slip it from the left needle to the right needle; remove it when no longer needed.

KNITTING IN THE ROUND
USING CIRCULAR KNITTING NEEDLES

When you knit a tube, as for a hat, you are going to work around on the outside of circle, with the right side of the knitting facing you.

Using a circular knitting needle, cast on all stitches as instructed. Untwist and straighten the stitches on the needle to be sure that the cast on ridge lies on the inside of the needle and never rolls around the needle.

Hold the needle so that the ball of yarn is attached to the stitch closest to the **right** hand point. Place a marker to mark the beginning of the round.

To begin working in the round, knit the stitches on the left hand point *(Fig. 7)*.

Continue working each round as instructed **without turning the work**; but for the first three rounds or so, check to be sure that the cast on edge has not twisted around the needle. If it has, it is impossible to untwist it. The only way to fix this is to rip it out and return to the cast on round.

Fig. 7

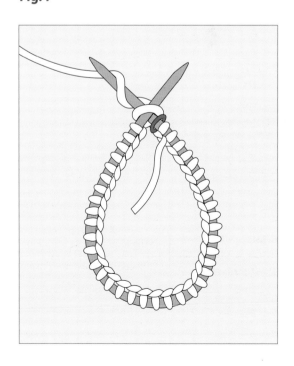

USING DOUBLE POINTED KNITTING NEEDLES

When working a piece that is too small to use a circular knitting needle, double pointed knitting needles are required. Divide the stitches into thirds and slip one-third of the stitches onto each of 3 double pointed needles, forming a triangle. Do **not** twist the cast on ridge. With the fourth needle, knit across the stitches on the first needle *(Fig. 8)*. You will now have an empty needle with which to knit the stitches from the next needle. Work the first stitch of each needle firmly to prevent gaps. Continue working around without turning the work.

Fig. 8

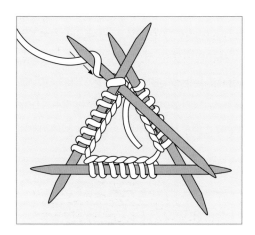

INCREASES
INCREASING EVENLY

Divide the number of increases required into the number of stitches on the needle. This number is the approximate number of stitches to be worked between each increase. Adjust the number as needed.

YARN OVER *(abbreviated YO)*

Bring the yarn forward **between** the needles, then back **over** the top of the right hand needle, so that it is now in position to knit the next stitch *(Fig. 9)*.

Fig. 9

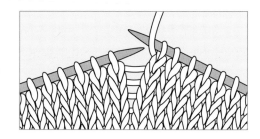

YARN OVER TWICE *(abbreviated YO twice)*

★ Bring the yarn forward **between** the needles, then back **over** the top of the right hand needle; repeat from ★ once **more**, so that it is now in position to knit the next stitch *(Fig.10)*.

Fig. 10

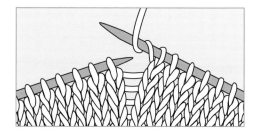

ADDING NEW STITCHES

Insert the right needle into the stitch as if to **knit**, yarn over and pull the loop through *(Fig. 11a)*, insert the left needle into the loop just made from **front** to **back** and slip the loop onto the left needle *(Fig. 11b)*. Repeat for the required number of stitches.

Fig. 11a

Fig. 11b

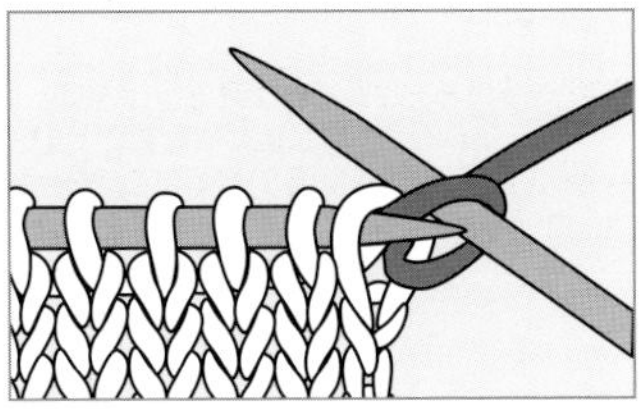

MAKE ONE *(abbreviated M1)*

Insert the left needle under the horizontal strand between the stitches from the **front** *(Fig. 12a)*; then **knit** into the back of the strand *(Fig. 12b)*.

Fig. 12a

Fig. 12b

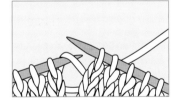
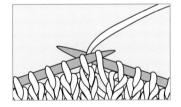

MAKE ONE PURL *(abbreviated M1P)*

Insert the left needle under the horizontal strand between the stitches from the **front** *(Fig. 13)*; then purl into the **back** of the strand.

Fig. 13

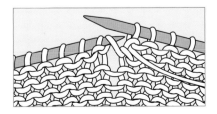

KNIT INCREASE

Knit the next stitch but do **not** slip the old stitch off the left needle *(Fig. 14a)*. Insert the right needle into the back loop of the same stitch and **knit** it *(Fig. 14b)*, then slip the old stitch off the left needle.

Fig. 14a

Fig. 14b

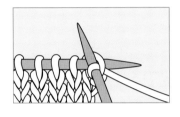
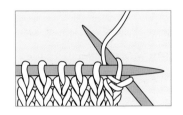

PURL INCREASE

Purl the next stitch but do **not** slip the old stitch off the left needle. Insert the right needle into the back loop of the same stitch from **back** to **front** *(Fig. 15)* and purl it. Slip the old stitch off the left needle.

Fig. 15

DOUBLE INCREASE

Knit the next stitch but do **not** slip the old stitch off the left needle *(Fig. 14a)*. Insert the right needle into the back loop of the same stitch and **knit** it *(Fig. 14b)* but do **not** slip the old stitch off the left needle, then knit into the front of the same stitch, then slip the old stitch off the left needle.

DECREASES
KNIT 2 TOGETHER *(abbreviated K2 tog)*

Insert the right needle into the **front** of the first two stitches on the left needle as if to **knit** *(Fig. 16)*, then **knit** them together as if they were one stitch.

Fig. 16

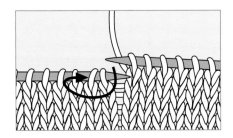

KNIT 2 TOGETHER THROUGH BACK LOOP
(abbreviated K2 tog tbl)

Insert the right needle into the **back** of the first two stitches on the left needle as if to **knit** *(Fig. 17)*, then **knit** them together as if they were one stitch.

Fig. 17

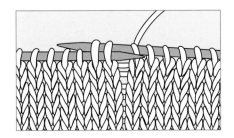

KNIT 3 TOGETHER *(abbreviated K3 tog)*

Insert the right needle into the **front** of the first three stitches on the left needle as if to **knit** *(Fig. 18)*, then **knit** them together as if they were one stitch.

Fig. 18

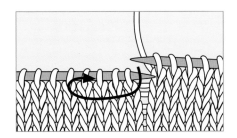

SLIP 1, KNIT 1, PASS SLIPPED STITCH OVER
(abbreviated slip 1, K1, PSSO)

Slip one stitch as if to **knit** *(Fig. 19a)*. Knit the next stitch. With the left needle, bring the slipped stitch over the knit stitch just made *(Fig. 19b)* and off the needle.

Fig. 19a   **Fig. 19b**

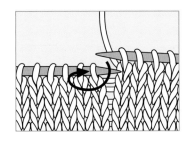   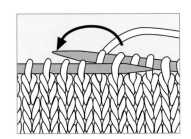

SLIP 1, KNIT 2 TOGETHER, PASS SLIPPED STITCH OVER

(abbreviated slip 1, K2 tog, PSSO)

Slip one stitch as if to **knit** (*Fig. 19a, page 30*), then knit the next two stitches together (*Fig. 16, page 30*). With the left needle, bring the slipped stitch over the stitch just made (*Fig. 20*) and off the needle.

Fig. 20

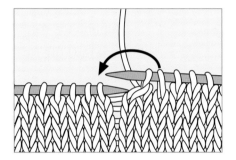

PURL 2 TOGETHER (abbreviated P2 tog)

Insert the right needle into the **front** of the first two stitches on the left needle as if to **purl** (*Fig. 21*), then **purl** them together as if they were one stitch.

Fig. 21

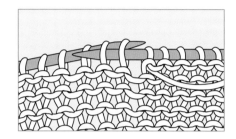

PURL 3 TOGETHER (abbreviated P3 tog)

Insert the right needle into the **front** of the first three stitches on the left needle as if to **purl** (*Fig. 22*), then **purl** them together as if they were one stitch.

Fig. 22

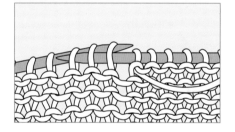

MEET THE DESIGNER

LISA GENTRY won the Guinness Book of World Records Fastest Crocheter certificate in 2005. There's another amazing side to Lisa—she designs entirely original crochet and knitting patterns, also at lightning speed!

When she's not creating for Leisure Arts publications, Lisa continuously develops fashions for well-known yarn companies. She also sells her own downloadable patterns and pattern collections on her Web site at HookandNeedleDesigns.com. She is a group moderator on Ravelry.com, where many of her designs can be seen. To collect all of Lisa's unforgettable Leisure Arts publications, visit LeisureArts.com.

Each project in this leaflet was made using Medium Weight Yarn. Any brand of medium weight yarn may be used. It is best to refer to the yardage/meters when determining how many balls or skeins to purchase. Remember, to arrive at the finished size, it is the GAUGE/TENSION that is important, not the brand of yarn.

For your convenience, listed below are the specific yarns used to create our photography models.

SEED STITCH BEANIE
Patons® Classic Wool
Grey - #00224 Grey Mix
Pink - #77402 Magenta

RIBBED BEANIE
Patons® Classic Wool
#00225 Dark Grey Mix

TWISTY CABLES BEANIE
NaturallyCaron.com Country
#0007 Naturally

LACY BEANIE
NaturallyCaron.com Country
#0005 Ocean Spray

BASIC BEANIE
Red Heart® Boutique® Midnight™
#1942 Serenade

CABLES BEANIE
Bernat® Mosaic
#44315 Ninja

NEWSBOY BEANIE
Red Heart® Soft
#9623 Spearmint

LACY HEADWRAP
Lion Brand® Wool-Ease®
#140 Rose Heather

CABLE HEADWRAP
Lion Brand® Amazing®
#202 Rainforest

SPLIT HEADWRAP
Patons® Angora Bamboo
#90532 Flamenco

Production Team: Writer/Technical Editor - Lois J. Long; Editorial Writer - Susan McManus Johnson; Senior Graphic Artist - Lora Puls; Graphic Artist - Stacy Owens; Photo Stylist - Brooke Duszota; and Photographer - Jason Masters.

Your opinion matters!

WE WOULD LOVE TO HEAR if our online video instructions and the new format of our publications are helpful to you!

PLEASE SHARE your comments and suggestions at www.facebook.com/Official.LeisureArts